LIKE YOUR LIFE DEPENDS

FIGHT

JON D. FORREST

randall house

114 Bush Rd | Nashville, TN 37217
randallhouse.com

Published by Randall House Publications
114 Bush Road
Nashville, TN 37217

Printed in the United States of America

ISBN-13: 978-1-61484-099-2

This book is dedicated to my incredible Bethel Free Will Baptist church family in Ashland City, Tennessee. I've worked with students there for a quarter century (good grief). Thank you for putting up with my cluttered office, horrendous closets of ministry junk, holes in the wall, stains on the floor, and countless containers of Nerf blasters. Your love for me and my girls is so dear to me.

TABLE OF CONTENTS

Preface vii

Introduction ix

    Week 1 Jonathan's Armor Bearer 1

    Week 2 Mary of Bethany 17

    Week 3 David's Mighty Men 33

    Week 4 Gideon 49

    Week 5 David the Shepherd 63

    Week 6 David the King 79

Note to Leaders 95

PREFACE

Let me give a special shout out to my Monday night men. You challenge me, inspire me, and make me want a cinnamon roll every time I think about you.

This is why this book exists.

Every Monday night at 7 o'clock, I meet with some pretty incredible guys at Bethel Free Will Baptist Church in Ashland City, Tennessee. We split up in groups and go out to our community to encourage people, deliver information about our church in cool little gift bags, and try to generally be a blessing without messing up *Monday Night Football* or *Dancing With the Stars* for them. When we are done some of us usually go to Golly G's for ice cream and giant cinnamon rolls. Depressingly, I just realized they may be showing up simply for the food.

My team is incredible. We were buddies before we were a visitation team. Jorden is a college freshman who has been part of this crew since he was in high school. My friendship with him is my last semblance of coolness. He keeps my handshakes lit and Hundo P. He also lets me know when it's time to stop using words like "lit" or "Hundo P." According to him, the time for me to stop using those words was when I was 21, but what does he know?

Aaron is the cool coach and P.E. teacher you wish you had when you were in high school. He's in his late 20's and you pronounce his name "Ay-run" which is really fun, like him. He's the kind of guy who, even 10 years after you've graduated from his class, you fondly remember and are still fascinated by his authentic dedication to your well-being. Also, at the time of this writing he's single, ladies! And he will try to gather up all the copies of this book and burn them because I said that.

It really is amazing how many people are watching *DWTS* on Mondays.

I think "Hundo P" is short for 100 percent. You know, "really good." If I'm mistaken and it's profane I apologize.

I've known Matt almost all of his nearly 30 years. He married an awesome girl. They've had an awesome girl. Matt is awesome. This is the transcription of the text he sent me May 3rd at 7:15 PM about an event he was helping me with. "Just tell me what you need. Where I need to meet you and when? And if I'm bugging you too much just punch me in the face haha." See? Awesome.

I've tried to find an engaging study we could read together. Unfortunately, we all pretty much hate to read. Now that I think about it, even if we liked to read we're not that great at keeping up with a book. We *are* good at some things though. We love to text. We love encouraging one another. We love the Lord and bragging on Him when we get to hang out. And although it has nothing to do with this book, we can also destroy some chips and salsa.

So I quit looking for a book for us to read and decided to write one—a book for people who aren't into reading. This is it. It's still probably a little wordy for a couple of these guys, but each day is about 500 words. That's about the length of a conversation you'd have with an old friend you run into in the beef jerky aisle at the gas station.

There are better books you could read, but none of those authors love you more than I do, nor are they cheering for you any harder than I am. I hope you will be encouraged, challenged, and maybe even mildly amused as you read it.

INTRODUCTION

Although I was sitting on the front row that night, I made the long nerve-racking walk to the altar to give Christ control of my life at the tender age of 6. My best friend had gotten saved that morning, and I didn't even like him going to Polar Freeze to get a Purple Cow without me. So I certainly didn't want him to go to heaven without me.

My parents tell this part of the story with glee. When we got home after church, I went to the kitchen, pulled a chair over to the fridge, climbed to where I could reach the little wooden switch my dad used to urge me to do the right thing, and removed it from its holding spot. I walked over to the trash can, broke it into pieces, dusted my hands off, and said, "Well, I guess we won't be needing *that* anymore."

My dad replaced the switch in less than a week.

I just assumed life went in a certain order.

You're born.

You wallow around in sin.

You get under conviction.

You get saved. In your face satan!

You live the life of simple and easy victory until God calls you home.

I was wrong.

How I'd love to go back and tell husky little Jon the real fight begins when you make your commitment to Christ.

Don't get me wrong. Salvation is victory. Death is swallowed up. God's Spirit lives in you. You are not who you were.

But think about the way Paul talks about the Christian walk. It's a fight. It's a wrestling match.

A "Purple Cow" is a grape milkshake that very well might change your life.

ix

I have good news though, my dear friends. You're up for a good tussle. Seriously, look at those fists. Don't let the recent manicure fool you. Those soup bones were made for a fracas.

I struggled with the subtitle for this book. If it were exclusively for girls I wanted to call it *Fight:"Wait, Somebody Hold My Earrings."* If you are not familiar with redneck etiquette, that is what a "lady" says before throwing fists with a fellow "lady."

I'm not advocating settling our disputes with our fists, but I am saying there are some fights that deserve our all. The fight to do what is right should be more intense that the fight over the last chicken tender. This is bigger than even fighting for your life. It's fighting to closer conform to the image of a holy God who fought and won the war for us.

The cool thing is you come from a long line of fighters. The people in this study make Rocky Balboa look like Strawberry Shortcake (the character, not the dessert). I hope you feel a kindred spirit with these people. Most of all, my prayer is that you will find a fresh burst of energy to FIGHT!

However, I will throw hands with you over the last chicken tender if there is some Chick-fil-A Sauce left.

WEEK ONE

JONATHAN'S ARMOR BEARER

Chewbacca, Pedro, Pumbaa, Samwise Gamgee. Can you guess what these characters have in common? Yes, they're all incredible, but more specifically they are some of the greatest sidekicks in history. This week we will focus not on a headline-grabbing hero, but a hard working sidekick.

Name a couple of your favorite sidekicks.

When Sam wades off into that lake to be with Frodo and he can't even swim, I weep.

Tonto, Robin, Art Garfunkel . . . the list goes on.

Good sidekicks are sold out to the idea of making their leader successful. They welcome blame and hard work and eschew credit.

Is your personality more conducive to that of the hero or the side-kick? Why?

Circle one:

HERO   SIDEKICK

I immediately aged 19 years when I typed "eschew."

How's this for dodging credit: Our fighting sidekick isn't even named in Scripture. He's just "Armor bearer." Can you imagine being known as "follower 1" in the movie credits of your life?

Before we get to our hero-follower let's take a look at the guy who should've been the hero.

Read 1 Samuel 14:2-3a.

King Saul, one of the two Israelites with a sword (it's a long, awesome story. See 1 Samuel 13:19-22.), was about 5 miles away from the fight in the "pomegranate cave" with 600 bodyguards and a priest wearing his church clothes. He was incredibly safe. There was a battle to be fought, but he was more concerned about avoiding confrontation.

Many of us are conflict avoiders. Are you more likely to face a problem head on or give it some space?

Circle One:

I face things head on.

I'm a chicken like you, Jon.

I understand. I'm a conflict avoider. I like to call it "being a peacemaker." The problem is there are some battles that need to be fought.

Sometimes in our walk we . . .

1. Avoid hard conversations
2. Neglect making the hard choices
3. Allow unhealthy attitudes to hang around for way too long (These blanks are for tough stuff you're avoiding.)
4.
5.
6.

Think about your most common prayers for a minute. Circle the one you are more likely to ask:

"Lord, keep me and mine safe."

"Lord, lead me into whatever fight you'll accompany me in."

Opryland was a music based theme park in Nashville, TN from the early 1970's to the late 1990's. I attribute its demise to the terrifying mascot Delilah Dulcimer who still haunts my dreams. Internet search "Delilah Dulcimer Opryland" before you scoff at me.

If your name is Baldwin and you're dating Isbell, I apologize. Those were the two most made-up names I could think of.

Think about it though, do you even *want* to sit around in safety eating pomegranates in your fancy clean clothes? Where is the adventure in that?

I was 17 years old before I rode my first upside down roller coaster. I was incredibly safe for those 17 years, but Opryland closed before I could know the thrill of riding the Wabash Cannonball. I HAD A SEASON PASS FOR TWO YEARS! Safety is not all that it is cracked up to be.

If a soldier finishes his battle and reports to his superior and says, "Sir, check this out. I made it all the way through the war and avoided every single battle. Never got a speck of blood or dirt on me." What would the general say?

Let's try a new prayer this week. Instead of "Lord, keep me safe," let's pray "Lord, I'm ready to fight any battle as long as You're with me."

As part of this time, take a look back at the list of things we sometimes avoid. You know, the list with, "Avoid hard conversations." Think about that list and write down a hard conversation you need to have. Some of these things are pretty personal. So possibly write it in code like this: instead of, "I need to talk to Baldwin about the way he treats Isbell" just write down "TTB." That's short for "Talk to Baldwin."

Hard conversation I need to have:

Sorry I didn't warn you yesterday. This is one of the absolute coolest stories in Scripture. I hope you are prepared for the pure awesomeness of Jonathan and his armor bearer.

While King Saul hung out in the safe, sweet pomegranate cave with 600 of his finest soldiers 5 miles from the battle, his son, Jonathan, grew increasingly enraged. Remember, due to the fact the Philistines had kidnapped all the blacksmiths, the Israelites only had two swords left. One was in the clenched fist of Jonathan who was staring down 20 of the baddest warriors Philistia had to offer, and the other was cutting open pomegranates in Saul's well-manicured hand.

Look at what Jonathan said when he reached his boiling point in 1 Samuel 14:6.

Circle the word in Jonathan's statement that would most concern you if you were the armor bearer.

"It may be that the Lord will work for us, for nothing can hinder the Lord from saving by many or by few."

If I'm the armor bearer, I stop listening at ". . . it *may* be."

There are several of these "it may be" moments in Scripture and history.

Remember when the three Hebrew children were faced with the fiery furnace and they gave Nebuchadnezzar a piece of their mind?

Shadrach, Meshach and Abednego replied to him, "King Nebuchadnezzar, we do not need to defend ourselves before you in this matter. If we are thrown into the blazing furnace, the God we serve is

In Saul's defense, pomegranates are delicious if you have $5 to buy one and can figure out how to crack into it.

5

able to deliver us from it, and He will deliver us from Your Majesty's hand. But even if He does not, we want you to know, Your Majesty, that we will not serve your gods or worship the image of gold you have set up.

DANIEL 3:16-18 (NIV)

The "even if He does not" in verse 18 is saying, "I believe the Lord can give me victory, but even if He doesn't, I still trust Him."

God does come through victoriously for Shadrach, Meshach, and Abednego. And (spoiler alert) He's going to give the victory to Jonathan and his armor bearer too. But as I'm sure you are painfully aware, God doesn't always swoop in to give the immediate victory. Yes, we who have made Christ our Lord have the *ultimate* victory, but there are some pretty serious losses along the way from time to time.

Consider the loss suffered by a group of missionaries in 1956. Jim Elliot and four other missionaries made contact with the Huaorani tribe in Ecuador. Due to the violent tendencies of the tribe, the missionaries slowly tried to gain their trust by lowering gifts from a circling airplane and communicating by way of a loud speaker on the plane.

In January of 1956, the missionaries had established what appeared to be a pretty good relationship by lowering gifts of things like rock salt, buttons, and even matches. The Huaorani people actually began to send gifts back up to the missionaries in baskets.

Finally, the missionaries landed their plane on a short strip of sand on the riverbank and made contact with the people. Tragically, a young Huaorani couple who were in the wrong place at the wrong time placed blame on the missionaries to cover for themselves. The tribesmen responded by spearing the missionaries to death on the banks of the river. The missionaries all died despite the fact that they had guns to defend themselves.

Be honest. Would you have used your gun when the men charged you with a spear?

What a loss! Young wives were waiting eagerly for word from the missionaries back at their base camp. They had done everything they could to

For a beautiful depiction of the story of Operation Auca, check out the movie, *End of the Spear* if you have a dump truck of tissues.

make this work successful. Surely the Lord was in their efforts. Still, the bodies of the missionaries were pulled from the river and buried in a common grave.

These missionaries must have thought, "It may be that the Lord will work for us, for nothing can hinder the Lord from saving, whether by many or by few."

After his death, in Jim Elliot's journal they found a quote probably inspired by the words of Philip Henry, a 17th century clergyman, "He is no fool who gives what he cannot keep to gain that which he cannot lose."

Although these men died, I think it's unfair to say that the Lord did not work for them. Two of the widows stayed in Ecuador and won many Huaorani to Christ, including some of the same men who speared their husbands to death!

Look at Jonathan's quote to the armor bearer one more time.

It may be that the Lord will work for us, for nothing can hinder the Lord from saving by many or by few.

This time circle the word *nothing* and read the statement again.

Whatever fight is scariest to you, is not impossible for Him.

What was Jim Elliot referring to when he said "that which he cannot lose?"

I know you are ready to get to the fight! It's coming. Actually, I think in this story there is a fight and then there's a less spectacular physical fight.

Read 1 Samuel 14:4-6.

Get the picture of this battleground in your mind. It might even be helpful to do an internet search of "Bozez and Seneh." It's a narrow but deep chasm with really steep rocky cliffs on each side. On one side is Jonathan and his armor bearer and one sword. On the other side is 20 fully-armed Philistine warriors with horrible attitudes.

An ambush is out of the question. Truthfully, it's impossible to even get to the other people without them simply kicking you off the cliff.

If you were in charge of coming up with an attack plan for Jon and AB, what would your plan be?

Did that plan stink? (Check one.)

❏ No, I'm a tactical genius.

❏ Yes, it was the worst plan ever. Even in a perfect world, they'd have been killed immediately.

Bozez and Seneh kind of looks like the Grand Canyon when it was in elementary school. It's the Bland Canyon.

Now come up with some possible attack plans for the 20 well-armed bad guys.

There are approximately 4,023 attack plans that would succeed for the Philistines. Like this one: "Okay men, there are 20 of us and 2 of them and they only have one sword. Hector, we are going to need you to take one for the team here. We will boost you up. They will stab you. This is kind of a vital part of this plan so don't miss this. When you get stabbed, grab the sword and fall backwards. Try to take Jonathan with you but if you can't, yell a little and make it dramatic. The rest of us will clamber up and beat them with all of our awesome weapons."

I mean, I'm not sure Hector is thrilled with that plan, but it's pretty foolproof.

We've looked a lot at verse 6. This is where the real battle is fought. This is where Jonathan asks the armor bearer whether or not he is in on this apparent suicide mission.

Before we look at the armor bearer's response write down 3 possible reasonable responses to Jonathan's question. At least one of your responses should include the phrases "I AIN'T GOT NO SWORD! Do you expect me to slap these guys to death with my shoe?"

1.

2.

3.

Sorry, Hector.

Memorize 1 Samuel 14:7 and let me know at jondforrest@gmail.com and I will let you know how proud I am of you.

Galatians 2:20 talks more about you being the walking dead.

When faced with the question, "Are you in?" pretty much every warrior in this book says something awesome. None of them answers, "I guess so." But out of all of these warriors we are studying, I like the armor bearer's answer the best. This dude is a warrior poet. Prepare yourself and then feast your eyes on 1 Samuel 14:7

And his armor-bearer said to him, "Do all that is in your heart. Do as you wish. Behold, I am with you heart and soul."

In your face, Shakespeare! **That's** a response.

When Christ asks you by His spirit, "Are you in?" how do you answer?

Sure, I guess   Yeah

Hmmm, Okay but . . .   Whatevs

Do all that is in your heart   Do as you wish

I am with you heart and soul

We don't even know this guy's name, but we just witnessed his death. It wasn't his literal death, but the rocky spot he was standing on at that moment might as well have been a gravesite. This is where he decided he was all in.

Dying to ourselves is a daily fight. Win it today!

Jonathan asked if the armor bearer was in for this suicide mission and his reply was *epic* (and I use that word sparingly and properly).

Do all that is in your heart. Do as you wish. Behold, I am with you heart and soul.

I don't know about you, but that makes me want to go punch somebody in the face, assuming they really had it coming like these Philistines did.

Draw a picture of what you think Jonathan's face looked like as he was asking the armor bearer if he was up for this seemingly impossible fight, and then draw what it looked like right after the armor bearer's reply.

Before   After

I've never punched anybody in the face. I used to think I'd be good at it, but once I let a criminal who was being chased by a policeman run past me at Dunkin' Donuts and I did nothing. So I'm afraid I might be a wimp.

I don't think it's wrong to think about the pleased look on Jesus' face when we go all in for Him. It's hard to tell someone, "well done" without an intensely pleased look. I hope that's what you are living for.

Read Jonathan's ridiculous plan in 1 Samuel 14:8-10.

How wonderful would it be to hear Jesus say, "Well done, _____ (Your name here) _____." I'm trying to live for that.

Don't you love it when those Philistines say, "Come up to us, and we will show you a thing," thinking they were going to wipe the floor with those two guys, but Jonathan and his armor bearer just hear a sign of their victory?

Any second thoughts if you are the armor bearer?

Jesus has some pretty counter-intuitive plans for us too. Read these peculiar battle plans. If people who fit these descriptions come to mind, write their initials next to the phrase.

Love your enemies. (Matthew 5:44)

Do good to those who hate you. (Luke 6:27)

Pray for those who mistreat you. (Matthew 5:44)

Bless those who curse you. (Matthew 5:44)

Yeah, I know. I'd rather fight 20 guys with no sword than do those things.

Continue reading 1 Samuel 14:11-12.

The Philistines are talking smack, but all Jonathan hears is the promise of God. This pre-fight yelling match reminds me of what happens at weigh-ins before fights. Sometimes fighters get intimidated to the point of defeat before the fight even starts.

If you're going to fight, it's vital for you to have a weapon. Our sword is the Word of God (Ephesians 6:17). If you have bought into the lie of not being enough to be used by God, grab these verses by the handle and swing away at the lies.

Circle the words you really need to hear today.

But the Lord said to Samuel, "Do not look on his appearance or on the height of his stature, because I have rejected him. For the Lord sees not as man sees: man looks on the outward appearance, but the Lord looks on the heart."

1 Samuel 16:7

See what kind of love the Father has given to us, that we should be called children of God; and so we are. The reason why the world does not know us is that it did not know Him.

1 JOHN 3:1

Then I said, "Ah, Lord God! Behold, I do not know how to speak, for I am only a youth." But the Lord said to me, "Do not say, 'I am only a youth; for to all to whom I send you, you shall go, and whatever I command you, you shall speak. Do not be afraid of them, for I am with you to deliver you, declares the Lord."

JEREMIAH 1:6-8

Read 1 Samuel 14:13-15 to see how the battle turned out. (Spoiler: it's awesome.)

Can you see this fight in your mind? I wonder how quickly the armor bearer got a weapon off of a dead Philistine. I kind of like the thought of him standing there as the last Philistine hits the floor, breathing hard with a broken off piece of shoestring in his hand, daring someone to get back up and get some more.

I love this Jeremiah verse. He sounds so much like me with that, "Ah, Lord God!" But God tells him to stuff those excuses in a box.

Can you remember from our reading what prompted Jonathan and his armor bearer to fight? (Don't waste a lot of your day on this. It's kind of a trick question.)

There are two words at the beginning of the 1 Samuel 14 that can sneak by you if you're not careful. The more you think about them the weightier they become.

Write down the first two words of 1 Samuel 14.

_____ _____

Six little letters. Two tiny words.

"One day."

It appears to me that on this one day, Jonathan got tired of looking across the chasm at an enemy who needed to be defeated, and on that one day he decided it was time to fight.

My construction buddy who helps me with church projects all the time told me how he quit smoking. He said, "One day, I just set the pack down and never picked them up again." He just decided he was done. It was a battle, but he made up his mind to fight it "one day."

Have you ever experienced the power of a "one day" and quit doing something or started doing something? Fill in the blank with it.

One day I decided _____

_____

_____.

One day I decided to eat right. One day I decided to stop hating Lacy. One day I decided to start readying a Bible study. What made you pick up this book and start doing a Bible study by the way?

Was it a person? Did you get it on sale at the secondhand bookstore? Are you a member of my family who was unfortunate enough to have me draw your name in our family gift exchange?

I'm not sure what it was that prompted you to read up to this sentence, but I'm so glad you did, because you are a fighter. If you're not careful you can forget *that* little fact and end up eating pomegranates in a safe cave all your life instead of fighting enemies that need to be defeated.

Hey, don't get me wrong, pomegranates are delicious. I'm pretty sure they're full of anti-oxidants. (Full disclosure: I have no idea what an oxidant is, much less an anti-oxidant. Basically, I watch a lot of commercials and oxidants seem to be horrible little things). But, as good as pomegranates are, they can't compare to standing on a cliff with your buddy, knee-deep in a sea of defeated enemies who had it coming.

Identify a battle in your life that needs to be fought. Is there a habit or attitude in your life that needs to die? Maybe the battle in your life is something that needs to start.

I know how tough these decisions to change are. People act like losing weight is so easy. Just eat less and/ or exercise more. "People" don't understand. I'm typing this 10 miles from a Chick-fil-A and it's way too early to be thinking about lunch, and yet I can hear those little sauce packs crying out my name from under the counter. It's a fight!

If this book was a gift from someone, please hug them for me.

15

I know I'm asking some of you to get out of your comfort zone by drawing, but this is your book. Just do your best. Draw two cliffs here. Put you on one of them and put the enemy on the other side.

I know you can do it. You're incredible. You made it through a week of this study already. You can do anything!

One day, when you're ready, cross over and show that thing who its daddy is.

The really cool thing is I checked the calendar and it just so happens to be "one day" today. That bad attitude may have seen its last morning in your life. Today could be the day pornography got punched in the face by you. Come on, Champ. Start swinging!

WEEK TWO

MARY OF BETHANY

Quickly write the names of three of your closest friends.

1.

2.

3.

If #1 was not Jesus, you are just the worst.

Sorry, I'm kidding. That was a trap. But honestly I hope you consider yourself a friend of Jesus. And although He does call us "friends," (John 15:15) the truth is most of us are too practical to consider ourselves friends with someone we've not seen in person, not to mention He is the King of glory.

Can you imagine being one of those friends who Jesus hung out with? I'm talking about being closer than just one of His followers. He had friends He enjoyed spending time with. Our next fighter is one of those friends. Some of you can really identify with her. Her first fight is with her sister.

It seems whenever Jesus went through Bethany He enjoyed staying with Mary, Martha, and Lazarus.

Read Luke 10:38-40a.

If I didn't make your list of your top 3 friends, just give it some time. I'm persistent and tend to grow on people . . . slowly and quietly like a mold. It only took me 25 years to wear down my wife to accept my proposal. By the way, now she is only mildly annoyed by me.

Visualize this. Jesus comes to your house to visit. Circle one. Would you . . .

Be running around making sure everything is perfect

Sitting crisscross applesauce at His feet

These are the two types of people in the world. I'm a "sitter," but I have always felt so bad for the "runners" when I read this story.

Go ahead and read verses 40-42 in Luke 10.

It's just us here. You can be honest. We know Jesus handled everything perfectly, but do you have to wrestle with how He is a little soft on Mary and hard on Martha?

Mary is sitting there.

Martha is about 3 seconds from saying, "Jesus, tell Mary to get in here and help me! This bread is not going to make itself! Oh and You might have a few of those disciples pick up a little in there while we are finishing up this casserole. Were y'all raised in a barn or something?"

Then one of the disciples, probably Peter would retort: "Well, it was more of a stable, but as a matter of fact…"

Be cautious here. This is not an attack on working, nor is it an incentive to sit around all the time.

It's apparent Jesus stayed with this family on more than a couple occasions, but if you added up all the time He was with them it was only hours, if not minutes. If there was ever a time to throw a couple unheated Pop-Tarts out on the table and take advantage of valuable time at the feet of the Master, this was it.

One of the most endearing things about Jesus to me is His ability to endure our questions patiently. Don't run from or cover over your questions of Him. Dig in and find out why He did things. He's never wrong. It's always for our benefit. Sometimes it's just hard to see.

What has been fighting for your attention while you've been reading this today?

Facebook	Instagram	Twitter	Tumblr
SnapChat	VKontakte	Linkedin	
Kids	Work	Friends	Hobbies

VKontakte is sort of a Russian version of Facebook.

Luke 10:40 says, "But Martha was distracted with much serving."

The Bible literally says Martha was distracted from the *best thing* because she was serving her Savior. If it is considered a "distraction" to serve a plate of health sustaining, delicious, life giving food to the God of the universe, can you fathom the importance of sitting at His feet to learn, enjoy, and appreciate Him?

What GOOD THINGS are distracting you from time at Jesus' feet?

Mary knew sitting at those feet was worth the fight. Oh, and if you think it wasn't a fight, you don't have a Martha in your life.

Read verses 41 and 42 again.

In your words, what is the "one thing" Jesus is talking about?

Let's get that "one thing" right today!

WEEK TWO DAY TWO

'll admit it's a bit of a stretch to classify today's installment in the "fight" category. Let's call it "Mary's fight for her brother's life." When you see how beautifully this reveals some of the character of Christ, you'll cut me some slack.

Read John 11:1-16 slowly and let verses 5 and 6 baffle you. Don't close your Bible. We are reading a lot today.

> *Now Jesus loved Martha and her sister and Lazarus. **So,** when he heard that Lazarus was ill, he stayed two days longer in the place where he was.*
>
> JOHN 11:5-6 (THE EMPHASIS ON "SO" IS MINE.)

In other words, Jesus loved these three so much, when He heard Lazarus was about to die, He did not go heal him. I'm not saying every bad thing that happens to us is Jesus telling us, "I love you; watch what comes from this horrible thing." But it did happen this time.

Once a quote becomes popular enough to be made into a pretty picture for easy posting on Instagram, I'm usually done with it, but I'm making an exception in this case. Mr. (Fred) Rogers famously said, "When I was a boy and I would see scary things in the news, my mother would say to me, 'Look for the helpers. You will always find people who are helping.' To this day, especially in times of 'disaster,' I remember my mother's words and I am always comforted by realizing that there are still so many helpers—so many caring people in the world."

He's right. There are many good people who help, and it's good to take courage from them. But as followers of Christ, it's criminal for us not to keep an eye out for *the* Helper. He is with us even in the "valley of the shadow of

Check out "Doubting" Thomas in verse 16. I think he should be called "Ready to Die Thomas."

"Overused quotes make me sick!"
—Jon D. Forrest

Feel free to tweet this.

death." What a horrible sounding place. Everything in our life, even that dark walk, is for His glory.

Take time to think of a recent struggle. Can you spot God's hand in it? Take a minute to write it down.

Read John 11:17-27 taking note of Martha's faith.

Read John 11:28-36 taking note of what Mary does when she sees Jesus.

This is a question worth spending some thought time on. Why in the world did Jesus "waste" time crying over Lazarus' death when He could have spent that time raising him to life? I mean, Jesus weeps, goes to the tomb (verse 38), is sad again, and then brings Lazarus to life. What is the deal with these tears?

(That wasn't a rhetorical question. Write down why you think Jesus was so emotional over a guy who was taking the equivalent of a really, really good nap by the time Jesus got done with him.)

The only explanation is Jesus is pained by death. In this passage, He is nearing His own "fight" with it. Death is the wages of sin (Romans 6:23). Commit sin. Earn death. Death is sin's ugly child.

Death and dying steal so much. That's one reason Jesus is crying.

This is so cool. Read John 11:38-44.

You may have heard this little anecdote preachers like to tell about this incident that I am not sure is completely accurate, but I still like it. In verse 43 where Jesus says, "Lazarus, come out," some people say if Jesus hadn't specified "Lazarus," all the bodies in the tomb would've come out.

I'm pretty sure if you have the power to raise the dead, you also have power to imply which dead man you are talking to without causing a zombie apocalypse, but it's not wrong to be awed by the resurrection power of Jesus.

Spend a minute or two thanking Jesus for winning the victory over death.

Perspective Alert This is the best illustration of the death of a Christian you will ever see. Jesus wept even though Lazarus's death actually only lasted the equivalent of a few thousand heartbeats. Death stinks. It's sad to see what sin has brought about. It's even ok to cry about it, but death does not win. One of these days I will take my final breath. But then, oh man, that next breath I take will be the fresh air of paradise.

So far, Mary has fought her sister and death. Those are both pretty formidable foes, but today she steps toe to toe with some cranky disciples.

Yes, I'm sorry to say some of our toughest fights can come from friendly fire. Keep this in mind when you're in a disagreement with a fellow believer, or anyone for that matter: being loving is as important as being right.

Before we begin reading in John 12, let's have a quick test. Based on what we've learned about Martha, what do you think she will be doing? Circle one.

This is worth a repeat in the margin. Being loving is as important as being right.

Serving   Yelling at someone else for not serving

Either answer is pretty safe.

What do you think Lazarus will be doing? Circle one.

Subject and predicate agreement is so peculiar sometimes.

Lying around dead   Lying around

Read John 12 verses 1-2.

How did you score on your previous test? Nobody has learned much, has he or she?

Here's a refresher on Mary's behavior.

From Luke 10-

"... Mary, who sat at the Lord's feet."

From John 11-

"Now when Mary came to where Jesus was and saw him, she fell at his feet."

Where do you think we will find her in John 12:3? Read and find out.

People are beings of habit. You probably did something today very similar to what you did yesterday. I hope reading this book is becoming a habit for you.

Envision the cool little bottle of this perfume Mary poured on Jesus' feet. In the next verse, Judas is going to enlighten us to its value. He's super concerned with money so I think we can trust his estimate. He says this stuff is worth 300 days wages. If you take out Sabbath days, that means this concoction is worth a year's wages.

Stop for a second. You didn't hear me. THIS GOO WAS WORTH $45,000!

If you dropped this book in shock and had to pick it back up to read this sentence, you are beginning to understand this unbelievable deed, but some of you still don't get it. So do this: Take out a $1 bill. Go to the restroom and flush it down the toilet. Do it. I'll wait . . .

How soul-crushing was it to watch that dollar circle the bowl before disappearing?

Now, GO AND DO THAT 44,999 MORE TIMES! Now you are beginning to feel what those disciples felt.

Verse 3 says the smell filled the house, but think about it. That was only momentary. She poured that ointment on His feet and it ran off onto the earth floor and no doubt made a small moist spot on the floor which got smaller and smaller until it became dry ground again. The smell that filled the house soon wafted out the window taking with it any evidence of the $45,000!

If your life depended on coming up with 45 grand by tomorrow, how would you do it?

The average American income at the writing of this sentence is 45 grand. Are you thinking you need a raise?

Don't really do it 44,999 more times.

I apologize for using "ointment" and "moist" in the same paragraph. They are two of the most hated words in the English language. At least Mary didn't set the moist ointment on a doily.

Today I want to leave you here where Mary and Jesus left the disciples. I hope your mouth is agape and you're a little confused, maybe even mad. Watch the perfume dry up on the ground. Notice the weakening of the sweet smell. Let the harsh reality of what just happened in front of you sink in.

Then think about these two questions:

Why did Mary do it?

Why did Jesus let her?

How'd you sleep last night? Were you tempted to get your plunger out and try to turn back time? If you struggled with the idea of the liquid version of $45,000 being poured out on Jesus' feet, you are not alone.

Read John 12:1-6.

It's usually not a good idea to side with Judas Iscariot, but when you read this do you kind of see where he's coming from?

Seriously, they could've sold this stuff and started a homeless ministry! Why did Jesus allow her to do this? Make sense of it.

Let's do a fill in the blank. This is why He allowed Mary to pour out a year's wages on His feet.

HE _____ WORTH IT!

Is is the word that fills in the blank. He IS worth it. And Mary knew it. I think she poured $45,000 worth of ointment on Him because she didn't have $46,000.

The truth is there is no sacrifice, no matter how vast, made for Christ that is too big or undeserved.

Hudson Taylor was a missionary in the late 1800's to the almost impenetrable country of China. Before he left home, he was in love with a girl whose parents would not let her go to the dangerous Far East, but offered Hudson a great job to stay. He did not. He left his love and a profitable job in ministry.

That was only the beginning. He suffered sickness, fire, theft, extreme poverty, death of loved ones, abandonment, and much more in his quest to introduce the people of China to God he loved. He absolutely emptied himself and still he said: "I never made a sacrifice. If I had a thousand pounds, China should have it—if I had a thousand lives, China should have them.

Every time I read this story I wonder if this time Jesus will stop Mary right before she pours the ointment and say, "Wait! Wait! Wait! I get it. You are dedicated. That stuff is worth $45,000 though. Let's dial it back a little here."

Read a few chapters in *Hudson Taylor's Spiritual Secret* by Dr. and Mrs. Howard Taylor. Warning: you'll probably want to name your kid "Hudson" or "Taylor" after getting a peek at that warrior.

"Indignant" is an awesome word. It means you are mad because of unfair treatment, which is an even worse look for these disciples. Try to slip it in a conversation today and secretly grin, knowing I'm grinning with you.

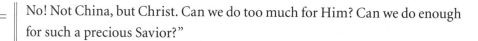

No! Not China, but Christ. Can we do too much for Him? Can we do enough for such a precious Savior?"

If Hudson Taylor was right that we could never make a sacrifice for Christ, what is the closest you have ever come to sacrifice for Him? How have you suffered to make Him great?

Was yours the sacrifice of a little money? Was it some kind of temporary discomfort? Did you have trouble of thinking of a real "sacrifice"?

Read this same story of Mary in Matthew 26:6-8.

The disciples were *yelling* about wasting this precious ointment on Jesus' feet. Look at verse 8.

And when the disciples saw it, they were indignant, saying, "Why this waste?"

MATTHEW 26:8

The disciples were almost mad enough to physically hurt Mary for "wasting" this small fortune on Jesus. Mary, on the other hand, looked at this Savior, the King of all creation who was about to die for her, and asked, "Jesus, why this waste? Why would the Lord of everything waste Himself on me?"

Spend some time thinking about Jesus' sacrifice for you and your response to this love.

Every word of your Bible is inspired and true. The chapter and verse breaks are not. I'm glad they are there. They help us all get on the same page literally, but sometimes they keep us from feeling the flow of a story.

Read Matthew 26:6-16 and try to ignore the verse breaks and descriptions.

One of the words in the ESV that stands out in these verses is "indignant." I hope you found a reason to use it in a sentence yesterday. On an angry scale, "indignant" is just before "completely losing your bacon." These guys were shakily furious. Mary's fight was almost a physical one with the disciples when she anointed her King. One of them seemed especially upset.

If Mary represents complete disregard for money and Judas is consumed by money, circle the number where you fall.

Mary   Judas

1   2   3   4   5   6   7   8   9   10

What is it about money that makes us lose our minds?

In the year 1244 Stephen Langton separated the Bible into chapters. I can't prove this, but I have a strong feeling his office was more organized than mine.

The fact that Jesus allowed Mary to anoint Him with this expensive perfume seems to be what pushed Judas over the edge. Matthew links the selfless act of Mary and the selfishness of Judas in his account. He gives us the impression Judas left this dinner party and went directly to the chief priests to sell Jesus out.

Before we get too mad at Judas consider this: He got 30 pieces of silver for the King of the Universe.

We trade Him for far less sometimes. Every time we choose disobedience or trade our time with Him for something "more important," we are selling Him out.

What are some lousy trades you've made for Him lately? (For example, you traded sleep for time you had planned to spend with Him.)

Judas saw the blind receive their sight. He was there the day a lame man leapt for joy when his legs were restored. The hands he used to gather the treacherous silver coins were once used to gather a basket full of LEFTOVERS from 5,000 people who had been miraculously fed with 5 crackers and two sardines. Days before the scene we see here, Judas had eaten supper with a guy he watched walk out of his grave after rotting for four days. Water to wine, coins in fish's mouths, walking on water, calming storms: Judas saw all this and more, yet he fought off faith in Christ. Judas was a fighter too.

If you're anything like me you'd give up anything for just a glimpse at even one of those miracles I just named. Before we get too jealous, pause and be thankful we live on this side of the cross and we have God's whole and perfect Word. We believe these miracles by faith. Fight the good fight of *faith*.

Read Matthew 26:13 again.

People value 30 pieces of silver at that time between $60 and $3,000. I'd lean toward a couple thousand.

30

Here we are 2,000 years later, still talking about Mary's sacrifice. How many people around her made and spent their fortunes on things that have turned to dust? She fought for a place at Jesus' feet and was blessed for it.

True or false: Only things done for Christ will last.

What will you do for Him today? Whatever it is, He's worth it!

WEEK 3

DAVID'S MIGHTY MEN

We are about to enter a sacred zone. These are David's mighty men. I mean, it would be one thing if they were Jon's mighty men. Mighty in my book is killing a spider with only one paper towel wadded up in your hand instead of spooling off half the roll so you don't accidentally brush against one of those minions of satan. It's one thing to be mighty to me, but these guys were mighty to mighty David.

That dude did not play. Look at what he said to a nine-and-a-half foot professional fighting giant who wanted nothing more than to feed him to the buzzards.

> *You come to me with a sword and with a spear and with a javelin, but I come to you in the name of the Lord of hosts, the God of the armies of Israel, whom you have defied. This day the Lord will deliver you into my hand, and I will strike you down and cut off your head.*
>
> 1 Samuel 17:45, 46a

He straight up told this champion he was going to chop off his head. This cat knows what mighty is.

True or False: People who use phrases like "straight up" or "this cat" are old guys grasping at coolness.

True   False

This is how incredible this week is going to be: The first mighty man mentioned in 2 Samuel 23, Josheb-basshebeth, killed 800 men with his spear during one battle AND WE ARE SKIPPING HIM!

I apologize for saying "straight up" and "cat." My slang words make me sound like a gangster from the 1930's.

Read 2 Samuel 23:9-10.

Full disclosure here, I have talked about Eleazar in this passage for years, and I've handled it completely wrong. I'm a very visual reader. When I read about an occurrence, I see it. Sometimes my imagination goes faster than facts.

I have called Eleazar the "Carpal Tunnel Guy" for years. I thought these verses said he fought so hard, when the battle was over he couldn't turn loose of his sword. I'd say, "Be like Eleazar. Hold on tightly to the important things and they become more and more difficult to let go of." Let me take this opportunity to apologize to the Lord, to Eleazar, and to my students for my misunderstanding.

The real story is way cooler and has an even better application.

Read the verses one more time and let the battle come to life in your mind. Grab something close to you that is "swordy" and hold it like you're Eleazar.

What do you think it means when the Bible says David and his men "defied the Philistines?"

We like to talk trash, don't we? Back in this era, instead of going on social media and making an ambiguous remark referring to an opponent like we do today, these guys liked to yell insults back and forth at one another across the battlefield. The only problem for Eleazar was, on this day, all the other Israelites ran away while he stood.

If Josheb-basshebeth's friends didn't call him "Josh" I'd be very disappointed. How do you kill 800 people with a spear? Every time I think about Josh, I envision him holding a spear with bad guys hanging from it like a skewer of shrimp.

The guy's name was Eleazar—son of Dodo. Pronounce it Dōdō all you want, this guy still had it rough in the third grade. It's no wonder he grew up tough.

What separates the runners from the standers?

We get a clue in 2 Samuel 23:10. Read it again.

He rose and struck down the Philistines until his hand was weary, and his hand clung to the sword.

If this were you fighting this battle instead of Eleazar, what would be the most likely statement behind that comma?

He struck down the Philistines until his hand was weary, . . .

_____ then he ran like a surprised lizard

_____ then he negotiated a surrender

_____ then he asked if the Philistines were hiring

_____ then he fell on his sword

Finish these more commonplace battle statements (overlooking the run-on sentences.)

Jon was spending time with God when things in his life got pretty busy, and then _____

_____ .

Marty was winning the war on porn in his life. He could hear the sites calling his name, and then _____

_____ .

Angelina drew lines in her relationship and the dude kept pushing the boundary, and then _____

_____ .

This comma in Eleazar's life is his defining moment. What will you do with your comma?

When we get tired of fighting, we usually make bad decisions. Think about the thing that is your greatest temptation these days. Write it down, but use x's instead of actual letters. This is pretty personal.

My greatest temptation is _____

_____.

Next time you are fighting this and you get weary, instead of giving in: pull an Eleazar. It's invigorating to fight until you are pooped and then to FIGHT SOME MORE!

We will see this same crop thievery when we look at Gideon. Do NOT mess with my food!

Spell check says I cannot use "mayo" as a verb. I'm going to leave it and see if my editor lets it pass.

How do you like your bacon? Correct answer: in your mouth. Even better answer: with a side of tomato-stealing venison.

Have you had any fights since we hung out? Did you pull an Eleazar and hold on even when you felt like giving in? Oh, I hope you held on. I'm praying for you while I'm typing this. I have a lot of regrets in my life, but none of them is from times I held on when I felt like giving up.

Our next mighty man is Shammah, the son of Agee the Hararite. It makes your name look so cool when you put it like that. Check this out. Greetings, I'm Jon, the son of Terry the Cheap Hillian. Yeah, that didn't turn out quite as cool as I thought since we were from Cheap Hill, Tennessee. But try it with your name _____.

Read about Shammah in 2 Samuel 23:11-12.

Bad guys throughout history have this practice of swooping in and stealing the good guy's crops just before they are able to enjoy their harvest. It's a terrible cruelty that is largely lost on us due to the fact that most of us harvest our produce from the front section of Walmart.

One year I had a couple of tomato plants. I'm a horrible farmer. I planted them in shade because I hated messing with them in the hot sun. Needless to say, they did not do well. However, I did finally have one beautiful Bradley tomato hanging proudly on the vine. As it ripened, I got excited. I bought a pack of bacon, which I skillfully fried up in the microwave, mayo'ed up some bread, and proceeded to the garden to harvest the fruit of my labor. To my horror, my tomato was gone. On the ground was a piece of tomato about the size of the salsa I drop on my shirt every time I go to a Mexican restaurant. As I lay weeping in my yard I can't be sure, but I'm almost positive I heard the thieving deer attempt to muffle his snicker as he watched from a safe distance. This I why I feel nothing when I watch *Bambi*.

When the Philistines gathered at Lehi, they were trying to pull this same stunt on Shammah. The Israelite men all ran away.

Have you heard of "fight or flight"? When your body perceives a sudden threat, all sorts of chemicals go to work to prepare you for one of those two things. When someone jumps out from the shadows and scares you, do you feel fight or flight?

Shammah stood alone in the field. Standing is tough, but standing alone is infinitely worse. Why is standing alone so tough?

Personally, I think there should be a third option: fight, flight, or pass out in a recently formed puddle.

I love the way verse 12 says he took his stand in the middle of the field and defended it. Deciding to do what is right no matter what it costs is at the core of being a true fighter. If you don't nail that down, it's hard to become the bruiser you ought to be.

I remember one time as a college student I was standing at the counter waiting to order at a fast food place that has a creepy clown mascot and has sold billions of burgers. There was a girl in front of me who had already ordered and was waiting for her food. Two boys were at a nearby table telling the girl she was attractive in a very teen boy way. She nervously smiled, but their compliments turned to vulgarity. My mind was racing with my options for action. She soon got her food, and I noticed her tears as she hurried to the safety of her friends. I basically chose that "pass out in a puddle" option I spoke of earlier.

I can't tell you how desperately I'd like another shot at this. Do you replay dumb things you've done over and over in your minds? This one haunts me.

Man, I want that moment back. I want to tell that girl I'm sorry. I want to tell those guys to chill, and if they don't chill I'm going to get my blood all over their clothes. I want to act. I want to do right. Even if it means being alone and possibly even getting destroyed, I want to stand.

Read verse 12 again and see if Shammah really was alone.

Stand for what is right and you will never fight alone.

Think of your most recent lousy day. Are you having to go way back in your memory or are you in the middle of one right now? These days come for all of us, but let's dig a little deeper in this hole. Can you put your finger on your worst day?

Let's take a moment to celebrate the fact that you survived it! Survival is a victory sometimes.

We are going to look at one of the worst days ever in the life of one of the world's greatest champions. No one is exempt from the stink.

Read 2 Samuel 23:13-15.

David is having a terrible day in 2 Samuel 23. He has apparently been sent running from Bethlehem by the Philistines. Luke calls Bethlehem "the city of David," but this group of hooligans has forced him out of his home base at harvest time. That's usually the best time of the year for any culture. It's pumpkin spice time for goodness' sake and David has been forced to drink the dirty wall drippings in a crowded cave.

To me it feels like it's close to bedtime and he thinks about home and all its comforts - namely the sparkling clear cup of water he enjoys. He's sick of this cave water. He's sick of sleeping on a rock while the enemy enjoys the comforts of his home. All this becomes too much for David and he cries out.

Read 2 Samuel 23:16-17 slowly. I think these guys earned our full attention.

Understand David wasn't really asking for a drink. He was bellyaching. If he had Facebook, he'd have said, "How's my day? Well, I'm stuck in a cave drinking mud while my enemy is going through my pajama drawer. Thanks for asking! I'd give my right arm for a drink of water from that well by the gate! #thirstyANDdisgusted"

He's whining out loud with men of action in earshot of him. These guys hear their king make a request. It's a ridiculous, impossible request that is obviously not expected to be taken seriously, right?

This cave still exists. Search the cave of Adullam and see why David was so down in the dumps.

Unfortunately for the occupying force of Philistines, these guys are fighters. All they hear is, "the King wants a drink."

Look at verse 16 again. How did the mighty men make their way to the well?

Sneak attack?

Ninja style? Unnoticed?

The word that describes the way they got to the well is the same word that could be translated "chopped" or "rent" or "split open." These guys, no, these "mighty men" as verse 16 puts it, fought and hacked their way through the Philistines to the well, filled a canteen or cup of some sort, fought their way back through the army of bad guys, and delivered the water to their king.

This is the question for today: How do you react to your King's requests? Specifically, these requests:

Be holy, because I am holy (1 Peter 1:16)

My reaction _____

_____

Go and make disciples (Matthew 28:19)

My reaction _____

_____

Let your speech always be gracious (Colossians 4:6)

My reaction _____

_____

Note the inclusion of the word "carried" in verse 16. ". . . drew water out of the well of Bethlehem that was by the gate and *carried* and brought it to David." You try fighting an army with two buddies while carrying a cup of water without spilling it. It's not convenient.

Take every thought captive (2 Corinthians 10:5)

My reaction _____

_____

A true fighter only needs a whisper from his or her king to demand highest obedience, but these are commands. Pick one of the things from the list above that is especially tough for you and fight and hack through the enemy today to please your King.

How cool is our next fighter? Let's just say if my daughter had been a boy, her name would've been "Miles." That's what my wife wanted and I would've lost, but if I'd have had my way, he would have been "Benaiah!" We'd have probably called him "Benny Boy." Thank goodness for a daughter.

Benaiah. Did. Not. Play.

Read 2 Samuel 23:20-23. Drink it in as if you were watching an action movie.

Verse 20 says Benaiah was, "a doer of great deeds." What an incredible description!

Circle the phrase that best describes you.

A doer of great deeds   **A worker of long hours**

A watcher of much Netflix   **A worrier of many worries**

A kicker of many chillaxes

I hope you are a doer. That is a great title. The impressive thing about him "doing" things is that the odds seemed to always be against him.

Look at the first part of verse 20 again. "He struck down two ariels of Moab."

This word "ariels" only appears twice in the Bible. Both places refer to this same incident. One translation of the word is "lion-like." I don't know about you, but my mind automatically goes to Wakanda or an old wolf-man movie when I think of lion-like men. I don't know what they were but, HE FOUGHT TWO OF THEM AND WON!

I'm only slightly ashamed to admit when a new *Great British Baking Show* comes out on Netflix, I'm a "binge watcher of much Netflix."

What's your first move if you find yourself having to fight two ariels?

I can barely wait until tomorrow. That lion in a pit is so crazy.

These statistics are always changing and not improving.

See *Raiders of the Lost Ark*.

Next up, Benaiah killed a lion in a pit on a day when snow had fallen. We are going to take a closer look at this tomorrow, but that's incredible. I don't want to be outside in snow; much less in a pit; much, much less with a lion! He should not have come out of that one alive.

Let's not forget the "handsome Egyptian" he defeated. "Handsome" probably means huge and awesome. He had a spear. Benaiah had a staff, which is a fancy word for stick. Benaiah took the other dude's spear and killed him with it.

The odds were stacked against Benaiah in each of these fights. Nobody in his right mind would have given him a chance in any of them. I hate to be the bearer of bad news, but the odds are against you, too.

Eight out of 10 men in their early 20's struggle with pornography. It's not much better for the ladies. Four out of 5 women struggle with self-image. It's not much better for the men.

I wish I could say 10 out of 10 Christians are in a fight for right, but truthfully, it would be a stretch to classify the gentle struggle many people put up against sin a "fight." As I looked up the statistics for pornography, I noticed many studies asked the takers what pornography was. It seemed instead of fighting sin, many people tried to redefine it so they would appear less guilty.

I'm sorry. The odds are against you. The world is a fallen place with more pitfalls than an Indiana Jones movie. The good news is victories are sweeter for underdogs.

I played baseball in high school. Well, I was on the team. I got the "Billie Award" my sophomore year. It was given to a player with spirit who would cheer loudly, usually from the end of the bench. My team was good, though. As we advanced toward the state tournament, we met a team from a much larger town full of college prospects. No one gave us a prayer to hang with them for a single inning. Then something incredible happened...they absolutely destroyed us! We got beat so badly even I got to pitch. The score was so lopsided they practiced bunting on me. I started trying to throw at them but they were too stinking fast for me to hit.

But do you have any idea how sweet it would've been if we had beaten them? Having the odds stacked against you can be a blessing. It should make us focus.

Embrace your underdog status. Defy the odds today. Fight! Dig in and win a tough victory against whatever sin has been getting the best of you.

We were the Monticello Billies. Yes, like the goat.

Yesterday we looked at Benaiah, we passed over one of his most incredible battles a little quickly.

Read 2 Samuel 23:20 again.

The last sentence of verse 20 is less than 20 words, but it is a whole action movie.

Don't you love walking around outside when it's snowing? Ahhh. The quiet. The stillness. The LACK OF MAN-EATING BEASTS!

Actually, I'm not a huge fan of snow. I'll never forget the snowy day (and by "snowy day" I mean snowy by Middle Tennessee standards, which means there were seven flakes) when I stepped out of my vehicle to buy bread and milk (and by "bread and milk" I mean bread and milk by my standards, which is Pringles and French onion dip). I stepped out of my car onto the one slick spot in the parking lot. I went one way, my feet went another, and the seam in my khakis went another. My small town will never be the same.

As I pulled myself up by the dangling seatbelt, I noticed my wife in the passenger seat crying. I said, "It's okay, Babe. I think nothing is broken except for my pants and a small patch of asphalt here." Then I noticed her tears were not tears of concern. They were, "I just witnessed the funniest thing I'm likely ever to see" tears. Yeah, snow stinks.

But this snowy day in 2 Samuel involved not only snow, but also pits and lions. Pits are literally the pits! They're terrible places. You get in them and you can't get out. And don't get me started on lions. Lions still, to this day, eat more than 70 people per year! That's the pits!

I'm not sure what version of the Bible you read this story from, but look at how the New Living Translation interprets the second half of verse 20.

Another time, on a snowy day, he chased a lion down into a pit and killed it.

2 SAMUEL 23:20B (NLT)

This is absolutely a true story, right down to the French onion dip.

If you like Benaiah, you would love *In a Pit with a Lion on a Snowy Day* by Mark Batterson.

46

Carefully fill in the letters of the following word according to the NLT.

"He _____ a lion"

Why would any sane person ever chase a lion into a pit? If the lion is in the pit, go home and celebrate. He will most likely starve in there. If you find yourself in this position, whatever you do, do NOT try to bury him alive. See: the story of the farmer whose donkey fell into a well. You'd also be crazy to chase him in there.

Benaiah was a warrior. He chased the lion into the pit even when he may not have needed to. He did more than run from evil. He chased good. That lion needed to die.

In your life what percentage of time do you spend doing the following:

_____ % Fleeing from evil

_____ % Chasing good

Disciples have done a poor job teaching believers the whole story of living the Christian life. "Don't cuss. Don't lust. Don't hate . . ." and the list goes on. Those things are true and important, but they are not our whole duty. Those are sins of commission. They are things we commit. We are just as guilty for things we omit. They are sins of omission. These are things we should be doing that we fail to do.

James 4:17 says, "So whoever knows the right thing to do and fails to do it, for him it is sin."

We have a tendency to feel like we are the star of a movie, and everyone we brush by is just an extra in our story. Next time you're on the interstate, pick out a car headed in the opposite direction and think about how intricate that person's life is. We have seven-and-a-half billion opportunities to be doers of good like Benaiah. Do not just be an avoider of wrong. Be a lion chaser.

The donkey falls in a well. The farmer hates to see him suffer so he tries to bury him by throwing dirt in the well. However, every time he throws a shovel of dirt into the well the donkey shakes it off and tramples it down. They continue this until the donkey is able to step out of the well. The farmer celebrates by eating the donkey. No, I added that last part.

47

Not doing right is just as wrong as doing wrong. That's confusing, but true.

Write down three things you can do today to get a little lion blood on your hands. You know, how can you be a Christ-like blessing today? Maybe it's sharing your salvation story with someone. Maybe it's paying for someone's coffee.

1.

2.

3.

Chase a lion today! Do at least one of the things you listed.

WEEK FOUR

GIDEON

About 500 years before Christ would lower Himself to be born to a young girl in Bethlehem, Leonidas was the warrior king of Sparta. A vast army of Persians were bent on attacking the free people of Greece through the narrow pass of Thermopylae. Leonidas, with his band of 300 Spartans (and a few thousand friends), took their stand. The Persian king Xerxes sent word to Leonidas that he could avoid certain death and enjoy a sweet life under Persian rule if he would simply drop his fierce, Spartan-crafted weapons. Leonidas replied, "Come and take them." Consequently, the fight was on.

Sure, Leonidas and all his men were killed, and the pass was taken by the Persians, but it was a Pyrrhic victory for the Persians. A Pyrrhic victory is a battle you win, but the costs are so great it actually feels like a defeat. This perfectly describes every argument every husband has ever won with his wife.

Leonidas' 300 were valiant, but Gideon's 300 were valiant and victorious. However, "valiant and victorious" is not how Gideon's story begins.

The Midianites were making life miserable for Gideon and his people. The Israelites were supposed to be "God's people," but they had begun to worship false gods.

Read Judges 6:1-16.

The Midianites were doing that terrible thing that was popular in biblical times of stealing crops right when they ripened. Gideon had salvaged enough grain for a biscuit and was hiding in a pit trying to process these crumbs. It's not a good look.

(Sorry, I'm about to change tenses here.) An angel appears to Gideon in this ditch as he endeavors pointlessly, and this celestial being says something incredibly peculiar.

Apparently Leonidas really had the conversation in which one of his soldiers said there were so many enemy arrows they would block out the sun. His basic reply was, "Good, we will fight in the shade."

He's no Gideon, but Leonidas was tough.

The Lord is with you, O mighty man of valor.

JUDGES 6:12

Seriously, write down what your response would be if an angel appeared to you right this minute and said those words to you.

Many people believe the angel of the Lord in the Old Testament is actually an appearance of the Lord.

Gideon is unimpressed. He basically says, "Oh, is that so? If the Lord is for us . . . what's up?"

The first words we hear out of Gideon's mouth are ones of transparent honesty.

When is the last time you doubted those words, "The Lord is with you"?

Don't be afraid to take your questions to God.

Was it in a time of loss of income? A loved one? Health? Hope? Sometimes it's tough to trust when you can't see God's hand clearly. We are just like Gideon. He's able to give the angel a history lesson of God's love. He's been faithful to so many in the past, but we need Him now.

Then we see Gideon's real doubt. He doesn't question God as much as he questions himself. When the angel tells him God is going to use him, Gideon is less than ecstatic.

Please, Lord, how can I save Israel? Behold, my clan is the weakest in Manasseh, and I am the least in my father's house.

JUDGES 6:15

Gideon had one good reason he couldn't do great things for God. Give me five reasons you can't be a champ for God.

1.

2.

3.

4.

5.

The Lord's answer to Gideon's doubt still rings true for you. "But I will be with you." v.16

It probably wouldn't hurt to memorize Judges 6:16. Make it the home screen on your phone for a week.

God is with me. What an incredible truth!

O n to day two with our hero Gideon.

When was the last time you did something heroic?

As I took my daughter to school this morning we came upon a car on its side in the ditch. There was a man rushing to the front of it as I scampered up to the scene. He said the lady was fine but she couldn't get out. We tried to pull on a tire to bring it to rest upright, which, looking back on it, was a terrible idea. "Let's see if we can pull this car over on us! Pull harder!" Although I'd estimate our combined weight to be in the 550 pound range we had neither the strength nor the stamina to pull it down. I said, "Let's go around and see if we can push it to get it upright." We easily tilted it back to its wheels. The thankful lady crawled out shaken, but unhurt.

There are 30 reasons my actions were not heroic. The whole thing took 3 minutes. I basically leaned my aforementioned weight on the roof of a car. The most compelling evidence of my non-heroism is the fact I checked the community Facebook page a minute ago to see if a lady was looking for two chubby guardian angels who helped her this morning. Real heroes aren't motivated by credit. They are motivated by righteous resolve. We are going to see it in Gideon's life.

When we left Gideon, he was in the middle of getting to know his new visitor, the angel of the Lord.

Read about the meal Gideon prepared and what happened afterwards in Judges 6:19-27.

I'm still waiting for the mayor to give me the key to the city.

53

The Lord is peace.
He is also tenacity.

The most interesting thing about this passage is not the invention of the microwave. It's the fact Gideon builds an altar and names it "The Lord is Peace," and then immediately is called to do the most dangerous thing he can imagine.

Which of these is a bigger priority for you? Circle one.

Peace   Obedience

Gideon is about to realize true peace is not the absence of difficulty. True peace comes from diving into a good fight and trusting God to be next to you through it.

Gideon's father, Joash, is one of the Israelites we heard of earlier who had turned away from God and focused his worship toward the false god Baal. Gideon's first battle is with the sins of his father. God asks him to tear down Joash's idols.

We all have baggage from the way we were raised. Some of it is good. Some of it is not so great.

We all have bag-
gage, but it does
not determine your
future.

What attitudes and behaviors, both good and bad, look a lot like those of your folks?

Would you say your parents' (or whoever raised you) influence was mostly positive or negative?

It is hard to break free from those old inherited traits. It's even harder to confront the people closest to us with their wrongdoings. When Gideon works up the nerve and tears down his father's false gods late one night, the people in town want to kill him. Joash's response is as cool as it is surprising.

Read Judges 6:28-32.

Joash wasn't dedicated to those false gods. He just needed to be confronted with his sin.

Do you have people close to you who are not walking close to God? Pray for them. Live a godly life in front of them. And when the time is right, confront them with God's love. This is tough stuff. Even brave Gideon waited until everyone was asleep before he went to work.

Let's take a cue from Gideon. He felt like it was worth losing a little sleep to make a difference in his family's life. (Of course it also seems like he did his work at night mostly because he was terrified of his father.)

Tonight, after everyone is asleep, spend some time praying for people close to you who could use a fresh glimpse of God. Write their names on the lines provided below. You might want to just use their initials. I know all of this is tough work, but if Jesus is who He says He is, this is the most important work in the world.

_____

_____

_____

_____

_____

Nothing is harder, nor more important, than talking to the people closest to you about eternal things. Speak the truth in love.

I t's only 9:30 AM and it's already been a long day. As I'm sure my editor can attest as she reads this, I've been up since about 4 o'clock this morning. One of my "students" (who is now almost 30 years old) left with her husband and two little boys to help start a mission work in Japan. They are incredible people. Neither of them would consider themselves the "preacher type." I think it's safe to say neither of them would consider themselves as the "missionary type" either.

They've always been incredible help to me. Anything I've built at church in the last 12 years that looks halfway decent probably had their hand in it. They're awesome, but they are not your prototypical missionaries.

They decided to follow the Lord's leading to the mission field one night when Daniel was looking at Facebook and saw a report of the work starting in Japan. Daniel showed Shelby the post and said, "You want to go help with this?" And this morning at 5 o'clock with their two- and three-year-old sons, they disappeared through the security checkpoint with tears in their eyes and resolve in their hearts to make a difference in Japan. Fighters!

How do you know when God calls you to do something? Do you get a sign from heaven? Is it just a feeling in your gut? We'll continue looking at Gideon today and see how he figured out what God wanted from him, and we'll see if his method is a viable option for us.

Read Judges 6:36-40.

If you knew God would answer by the fleece method would you use it?

★★

We gathered around the altar to pray for them yesterday. If you would have heard the way their two-year-old said, "Papa" yesterday to his grandfather, who was kneeling in prayer for them, knowing he was about to hug him for the last time for two long years, you'd see what a real fighter looks like.

What would you ask? Fill it in: "God if you want me to _____
_____ make this fleece wet and the
ground around it dry."

This fleece method of hearing from God would be so handy, wouldn't it? What are the disadvantages of the fleece method?

Look at the last part of verse 37. Gideon is so human. Circle the phrase that should've given Gideon pause if he had realized what he was saying.

> *If there is dew on the fleece alone, and it is dry on all the ground, then*
> *I shall know that you will save Israel by my hand, as you have said.*
>
> JUDGES 6:37B

God had already said it. Gideon not only wanted a sign. He later wanted the opposite sign just to rule out some kind of magical dew.

God has also spoken to us through His Word. He wants you to take His name to a lost world. You don't need a sign.

I know what some of you are thinking, though. "Does He want me to go to Japan or Jonesboro?" "Does He want me to be a mayor or a missionary?"

Quickly, let me give you three guidelines I've used when pondering these really big questions.

Aren't you glad God is patient with us doubters?

No matter what your plans are, **do the next right thing.**

1. Where is the need? Look at your heart. For whom does your heart break? Discover where you could be best used.
2. What are my gifts? God made you with strengths. Embrace them. Don't dwell on your weaknesses.
3. What is your desire? If it were up to you, how would you serve? Psalm 37:4 says, "Delight yourself in the Lord, and He will give you the desires of your heart." If your heart beats with God's heart, you will want the same thing He wants.

Answer those three questions. Are you doing what God wants?

1.

2.

3.

B efore we read today, I want to give you a few numbers so you can better understand our warrior friend Gideon.

Gideon has 32,000 soldiers with him. That seems like a respectable fighting force until you find out there are so many Midianites opposing Gideon they look like a swarm of locusts. We find out later there were about 135,000 of them. I'll do the math for you. That's 4.21875 Midianites for every one of Gideon's soldiers. Not to mention their camels were uncountable, although Gideon and his servants estimated their number to be approximately the same as the grains of sand on the shore. Let's just say the Midianites live in a camel-rich environment.

Read Judges 7:1-8.

God wants to make a point with this battle. Look at verse 2. God does not want the people to say "_____ _____ has saved me."

I love self-sufficient people who work hard, but they have a lot of trouble accepting help sometimes, even help from God. If you are saved, you came to God with nothing but your sin in your hands. If any part of your testimony claims, "My own hand has saved me," you are not saved.

God did not want this point lost on Gideon and his men.

Read Judges 7:19-22.

What a cool fight! When I was in the 4th grade we had this little insult we enjoyed when we were trying to intimidate one another. We'd say, "If we fight, there's gonna be two hits: me hitting you and you hitting the floor." In this battle there were two hits. Gideon hit his pitcher and the Midianites hit the ground! Sorry, that saying sounded way cooler in 1982.

There is something fascinating about this fight to me. Imagine with me for a second. You are Gideon's fighter #213. You heard his crazy instructions. In your left hand you hold a warm pitcher with a torch flickering away inside begging to break the blackness of the night. In your right, you hold a trumpet.

If you had known me in the fourth grade you would've wanted to beat me up. And you totally could've.

Full disclosure: on a normal day for me, my jar is approximately the #294th to break.

I really like this paragraph. Will you read it again for me?

You've blown one before; although it wasn't very melodious, it was incredibly loud. Realizing Gideon may give his signal for you to break your pitcher and blow your horn at any moment, it hits you. "If I follow these instructions, 135,000 mad Midianites are going to pinpoint my location in approximately 0.2 seconds. The odds are now 450 to 1 in their favor and that's not even counting the camels." Your stomach churns, hoping against hope Gideon has come to his senses and decided against this ridiculous plan…From the darkness you hear "TOOOOOOOOT! FOR THE LORD AND FOR GIDEON!"

How long do you wait before breaking your jar?

This seems to be the way most of the fights we fight for God go. Sure, God absolutely gets the full credit for the victory, but there comes that moment where we have to decide whether we are in or out. Remember Jonathan's armor bearer in 1 Samuel 14:7? Or what about Mary in Luke 1:38 when the angel asked if she was willing to parent Jesus and she said, "Behold, I am the servant of the Lord; let it be to me according to your word." Or when my buddy Daniel looked up from Facebook to ask Shelby if she wanted to go help start a church in Japan.

None of these people regretted being "in." What about you? Are you on the fence in your commitment to God? It's a great day to sell out.

BREAK THE STINKING JAR!!

WEEK FOUR   DAY FIVE

I think Gideon and I would have been great friends. We have a lot in common. He's a scaredy cat who wants God to tell him every little aspect of every plan He has for his life. Then he wants God to say it again a little differently so he can be sure he is absolutely positive and there are no surprises. His faith, like mine, is tiny. What's something tiny I could compare it to? It's the size of a bean. No, what's something smaller? My faith is the size of a mustard seed. That's the size of the period at the end of this sentence! It's pitiful, but at least I'm in good company.

We skipped over a neat part of this story. Let's back up to the night Gideon and his 300 attacked the Midianites and the Amalekites. Gideon has already met an angel/short-order cook, taken the fleece test, and heard the voice of God telling him he needs to fight. It seems like he starts having a few doubts when God whittles his army down to 300 men.

Read Judges 7:9-15.

Compare yourself to Gideon. Put a check next to the statement where you would've been ready to fight.

___A. When the angel mysteriously cooked those cakes, I'd have been ready to rumble.

___B. After the angel and wet fleece and the dry ground, I would've whipped somebody.

___C. After the angel and the wet fleece and the dry ground and then the dry fleece and the wet ground, I would have messed somebody up!

___D. After the angel, both fleeces, and the interpreted dream, I'd have been a mean motor scooter.

I put an exclamation point at the end of that sentence after I talked about it ending with a period just to mess with you.

Being afraid doesn't disqualify you from being a fighter. A little fear sometimes comes with the territory.

I'm just so, so sorry in general if you have a gluten allergy.

Just a glimpse of this God should make us want to worship Him forever. He knows me and still, He loves me. Full disclosure: I may have left a couple of zeros out of the number of stars. But in my defense, scientists increase this number so regularly I can never keep up. Believe me, God holds them all in place and I can't even hold my socks in place.

____ E. Even after all that, I would still have wanted God to write me a message in the sky.

God was so patient with Gideon. In verse 9, God tells Gideon to go down to the enemy and beat them. Verse 10 begins by God saying (in my words), "But if you are afraid to go down to fight, go listen to what they are saying." Wait a minute. First, all 22,000 of the guys who were scared went home in verse 3, right? No, there was still some fear in the camp. Fighters are afraid sometimes, but they fight anyway.

Second, God gives Gideon one more sign. When he sneaks down to the camp, he hears one of the Midianites telling his buddy about a dream he had. I've had some weird dreams, but this one is outrageous. Basically the guy tells his buddy he dreamed a giant biscuit came rolling into camp flipping over tents and flattening the camp. His buddy doesn't even hesitate. He says, "Oh no! That's Gideon coming for us. We are toast!" I'm so sorry for all the bread references especially if you have a gluten allergy.

Look at verse 15 and fill in this blank. "As soon as Gideon heard the telling of the dream and its interpretation, he ____ _____."

It seems upon hearing this dream and its interpretation Gideon is convinced of God's greatness. When he gets a good look at God, he worships. Gideon didn't break into song. He didn't pull out a scroll and begin reading and teaching in a way we usually think of as worship. There wasn't necessarily any visible action that took place. At this stressful, pivotal moment, Gideon gets a glimpse of God, and Gideon's spirit embraces the worthiness of God.

It was one of those "God is incredible and I adore him," moments. Those moments don't come often enough. Think about this: God is holding more than 1,000,000,000,000,000,000,000 stars in place and still has plenty of time to "rejoice over you with gladness," according to Zephaniah 3:17.

Meditate on His greatness (His immensity) and His goodness (how He loves you) and worship Him.

WEEK FIVE

DAVID THE SHEPHERD

I f you are reading a book about biblical fights and David and Goliath are not mentioned in it, you've been cheated. What a story!

The unknown, overlooked shepherd boy goes up against one of the greatest fighting champions of all time. I'm not going to spoil the end yet, but I promise you it will be a knockout (foreshadowing pun intended).

But let's start at David's beginning.

Read 1 Samuel 16:1-7.

What would you guess Samuel saw in Eliab that made him think, "This guy *must* be the guy the Lord wants?"

When the Israelites chose Saul to be their king it seems his best qualities were his looks. 1 Samuel 9:2 (NIV) says, "Kish had a son named Saul, as handsome a young man as could be found anywhere in Israel, and he was a head taller than anyone else."

Where do you fall on this spectrum of looks?

I look like an old rusty shovel   **I'm Paul Newman (or the Female equivalent)**

By the way, if you're a guy, move your rank down 3 notches, and girls, move yours up 4. That's probably a little more realistic.

1 Samuel 16:7 tells us man cares about the outward appearance and we absolutely do. God is not distracted by the window dressing. He looks straight to the heart. What is He seeing in your heart today?

If you have ever thought, "There is no way God can use me," you are in good company.

Read 1 Samuel 16:8-13.

I searched "best looking person of all time," and Paul Newman was the top response. I didn't make the top 7 billion.

It seems like they almost forgot David even existed. They went through seven sons and none of them was called to be king. It's almost like Jesse says, "That's all my boys. Well, I guess if you count David I have one more, but there's no way it would be him. He's really more of a servant than a son."

Why would God use little David whose only gift is faithfully watching the sheep? I mean, he's not bad with a slingshot, but unless you're going to be attacked by a stray dog he's basically useless, right? Actually God has a tendency not only to use the weak to bring Him glory, but also He seems to use weakness itself. Things that would have made great excuses turn into God's glory: Moses' speech, Paul's past, Peter's attitude, Abraham's doubt, Jon's dislike of reading.

Write down three of your favorite excuses. It could be something like your fear of people or perhaps the horror of something in your past.

1.

2.

3.

Do not be surprised if God turns one of those things into something to glorify Him.

Imagine being converted right before beginning a prison sentence. Obviously you'd be thankful for your salvation but you would probably think your potential to minister to people would be gone. Not if you are Chuck Colson. After being released from prison for his involvement in Watergate, he began Prison Fellowship, the world's largest outreach to prisoners, ex-prisoners, victims, and families. His impact on the kingdom of God, which came as a direct result of his worst moment, cannot be measured.

You have a role to play in the kingdom of God.

Even the looks I've been dealt didn't prevent you from picking up this study and reading it. You would not believe how many filters we used on the picture on the back of this book.

One of my best friends in the world is 6'10". Donnie has to duck to get through doors. Sometimes when we are playing around he grabs me by the top of my head and almost accidently kills me. He's ginormous. Goliath was Donnie plus another half Donnie on top of that!

Get a pole and hang two gallons of water on the end of it. That's not a spearhead. That's a lawn mower engine on a stick!

I n 1989, when I was in 9th grade, I went to an Arkansas Razorback basketball game. They had a center at that time named Oliver Miller. His nickname was "Big O," and it was well-earned. He was 6 feet 9 inches with no shoes on, and well over 300 pounds before breakfast. I walked down by the court during warm-ups and stood close to him. I have no idea how anyone ever got a rebound over him. I'm positive my entire junior high basketball team could fit into his jersey at the same time. He was the biggest human I've ever stood beside. And Goliath would make him look like a kid.

Read 1 Samuel 17:1-11.

Get a picture of this guy in your mind.

He's roughly as tall as a regulation basketball goal with the bonus height of the finest helmet the resourceful Philistines had to offer. He was wearing 125 pounds of bronze body armor. Did you get that? His bullet proof vest was like wearing an eighth grader! The head of his spear weighed 15 pounds. How much is 15 pounds? The internet just told me it is 2 gallons of water, or a house cat, or an eagle carrying a 4 pound bag of sugar in its talons. That's a big spearhead. He also had a full body shield carried by a shield bearer. It would have to be bigger than a 4 foot by 8 foot sheet of plywood to cover this monster.

Draw a few of these things I've mentioned to begin to understand the fear Saul and his men must have felt.

Verse 11 includes Saul in the group of scared soldiers. Remember, he was head and shoulders taller than any other Israelite, but he was having none of Goliath either.

According to verse 11 they were "dismayed and greatly afraid." Looking at their enemy instead of looking at their God, they were scared and hopeless.

Dismay is that feeling where you are so overwhelmed you don't even want to get out of bed. Losing sight of God will put you there.

Read 1 Samuel 17:12-20.

It seems David was probably early middle-school aged when he was anointed by Samuel and maybe early high-school aged when he fought Goliath. He was too young to be a soldier and still looked like a boy to the Philistines. He was a kid.

Jesse made 10 cheese pizza Lunchables® and sent David to deliver them. Keeping in mind David was around 15 years old and the fact that he had been a little errand boy his whole life, read verse 20 and circle two stand-out things about David.

And David rose early in the morning and left his sheep with a keeper and took the provisions and went.

1 SAMUEL 17:20

He got up early.

I spend lots of time with 15-year-olds. They are a diverse group with varied talents and interests and personalities. The one thing almost every 15 year old has in common is the hatred for rising early in the morning. It's not their fault. They are growing. Their bodies need rest.

Also you may have noticed 15-year-olds tend to make strange decisions. There is a physiological reason for this. The part of their brain behind their forehead is not fully formed. I don't want to get all "sciencey" on you, but their decision maker is off.

David overcomes all of this in verse 20. He does the little things. He arranges a substitute shepherd. He gets up early. Little things make a big difference. How are the little things in your life?

Many physicists feel so strongly about the unformed pre-frontal cortex being responsible for bad decisions that they are working feverishly to have incarcerated teens released.

Some of my despised responsibilities are _____

_____

Because I despise _____ **sometimes I**

_____

Here's my real life example.

One of my hated responsibilities is going to the grocery store. (I love eating, but shopping and putting away groceries is about as fun as going barefoot cactus stomping.)

Because I despise grocery shopping, sometimes I make my whole family miserable the entire evening.

These little attitudes lead to actions. Maybe you've caught yourself having a shorter and shorter fuse around the people you love. Maybe you've noticed yourself becoming less likely to turn off a show that's a little more risqué than you would have been comfortable with in the past. Let's get a hold of some of these small things we've been letting slip by.

My dad is the smartest guy I know. Last week he told me, "People don't fall away. They fade away." Decide to fight fading today. Tighten up your game, love people, love God, and do right.

Online grocery shopping and pick up may have saved my marriage.

My dad is so stinking smart.

Yesterday David left his sheep with a keeper, got up early, and delivered some grilled cheese sandwiches to his brothers. Did you do better with your little things yesterday?

Read 1 Samuel 17:21-30.

Nothing's quite as sweet as the support of a loving brother, huh? Wow! Thanks Eliab. Only an older brother could come up with something this cutting this quickly.

"Why have you come down? And with whom have you left those few sheep in the wilderness? I know your presumption and the evil of your heart, for you have come down to see the battle."

Keep in mind the truth of the old saying, "Hurt people hurt people." Eliab was feeling a little wimpy and just took it out on the nearest easy target. Hurt people will do that to you, too. Eliab thought, "How can I put this guy in his place? Oh yeah, I'll remind him who he really is: a worthless shepherd boy." Fortunately for David, he knew who he really was. He was a fighting child of God.

Verse 30 is so important. Read it one more time.

How different would the story of David and Goliath be if, instead of saying, "And he (David) turned away from him (Eliab) toward another," it said, "And David ran behind a rock and pouted?"

Sibling put-downs are so natural. I love my sisters, but at this very moment I could come up with no less than 47 things that would for sure make them cry.

You can't control the jerk. You can only control the knee-jerk. (As in your "knee-jerk" reaction.) I'm not sure this makes sense, but it's really catchy.

When someone is a jerk to you, what is your "go to" response?

Pout   Call them terrible names in my mind

Punch their eye   Punch their nose

Turn away from them   Call them terrible names out loud

Another option you wish to add _____

_____

David knew this was a small person being small. People like that only have as much voice as you give them. Try turning away when you run into Eliab.

Read 1 Samuel 17:31-39.

I love the way David looks back at his past victories. He makes it clear that it was the Lord who delivered him from the lion's paw and the bear's jaw and God would deliver him from this giant, too.

Has the Lord been faithful to you? I have no doubt you have been through difficult things, but looking back on them can you see God's faithful hand? I imagine you can. But even if you can't, He was there. Do like David. Trace His hand in some of your past victories.

It's a little amusing to see the way Saul responded to David's talk about the faithfulness of God. Look at verse 37 and the first part of 38.

"And David said, 'The Lord who delivered me from the paw of the lion and from the paw of the bear will deliver me from the hand of this Philistine.' And Saul said to David, 'Go, and the Lord be with you!' Then Saul clothed David with his armor."

Saul was like, "Yes, David, God will take care of you…but before you leave, just to be on the safe side, let's pile this huge armor on you."

Saul is still trusting armor. David knows better. Listen to what he says in Psalm 20:7.

"Some trust in chariots and some in horses, but we trust in the name of the Lord our God."

Don't get me wrong. David is going to take his slingshot with him, but

Oil the wheels on your chariot, but TRUST in the Lord.

that is not where his trust lies. Trust God. Do your best. Don't be weighed down by someone else's armor that doesn't fit you.

No one can expect more than your reasonable best. My dad quotes his mom and grandma all the time, and most of the time I have no idea what it means until he explains it to me. For example his grandmother used to say, "Do your best. That's all a mule can do." Stay with me. He said it means once you do your best, that is good enough.

Trust God. Do your best. Breathe.

Coming to the understanding that your best is good enough is a big step in becoming wise.

Mine would be sharpened pointy orbs of death.

When I was little I remember one of my teachers said they heard David picked up five rocks because Goliath had four brothers. Although that makes me grin, I'm pretty sure that has no biblical foundation.

Did you feel something special in the air when you woke up this morning? It's giant killing day. This guy has it coming. The Bible talks about Goliath defying God. That phrase can be interpreted to mean Goliath intended to expose God for whom Goliath really thought he was.

Think of it like this, Goliath's defiance was making the point that these Israelites talked a big game about the power of their God until they were faced with a giant champion. "If your God is so awesome, prove it."

They proved how big they thought He was every one of those 40 days they peered around rocks, perhaps waiting for Goliath to die of old age.

Read 1 Samuel 17:40.

Five. Smooth. Stones. I assume smooth stones come out a slingshot better, but I still might go with a spiky one. Do you wonder why David only chose five or do you wonder why he chose so many? Draw the rocks you would've chosen for this battle in space below.

There was not enough space there for the number of rocks I would've chosen. I'm not sure if you are familiar with the snowball fight scene from the movie *Elf*, but that's what I envision my rock slinging would've looked like.

Read 1 Samuel 17:41-47.

GOLIATH:	DAVID:
Shield	"Mary had a little lamb" style staff
Sword	Glorified shoestring
Javelin	5 pebbles
Spear	Lord of Hosts
Shield bearer	
Armor	
Helmet	
Sheer enormity	
Brobdingnagian body odor	
(although I cannot back	
this up biblically, you can't	
prove me wrong)	

When you compare these two arsenals, it doesn't look great on paper for David.

That last sentence of verse 47 is haunting. "For the battle is the Lord's, and He will give you into our hand." The battle is the Lord's. David was pretty good with that slingshot, but he was not trusting in his aim.

What is the battle of your life right this minute? Illness? Job stuff? A cranky person?

Don't forget the battle is the Lord's. I know that seems to oversimplify very difficult things, but life really does come down to whether or not God really is the God He claims to be. Let's ask Goliath what he thinks.

Read 1 Samuel 17:48-54.

The writer of 1 Samuel has a knack for describing battles. "The stone sank into his forehead, and he fell on his face to the ground." After days of bravado you know every soldier on each side of the valley of Elah was straining his eyes to see this bloodbath. I'd say the only person not surprised by this outcome was David.

Brobdingnagian is an adjective meaning gigantic, based on a land in *Gulliver's Travels*. Use it in a sentence today and make it your own.

How cool is it that in verses 48-49 it seems that David almost forgets to even put a stone in his slingshot? I mean, I know the battle is the Lord's but why would you wait that long to pull a stone out of your bag?

Create an emoji to symbolize the feeling on the Philistine side when their giant's huge face went nose first into the dust in that valley.

Create an emoji to represent the feeling of the emboldened Israelites as David pulls the huge sword from the giant's sheath to finish the battle.

The bigger they are . . .

WEEK FIVE
DAY FIVE

What a fight! I'm tempted to say, "What a fighter!" But I'm not sure David would agree if I were referring to him. These words he spoke to Goliath were the last thing to go through the gargantuan's mind...well, next to the last thing. (I'm so sorry for that.)

> *This day the Lord will deliver you into my hand, and I will strike you down and cut off your head. And I will give the dead bodies of the host of the Philistines this day to the birds of the air and to the wild beasts of the earth, that all the earth may know that there is a God in Israel, and that all this assembly may know that the Lord saves not with sword and spear. For the battle is the Lord's and He will give you into our hand.*
>
> 1 SAMUEL 17:46-47

David lets everyone know, "the battle is the Lord's." That's kind of the point of defeating Goliath. It's not just killing a giant. Look at the last statement of verse 46 and the first seven words of verse 47. David wants to make the real champion known. The trophies he takes from Goliath are not to make himself famous.

Think about your trophies. List any of them that come to mind.

Actually, I'm sorry I'm not sorry. I love that crude, childish joke.

Yes Billies, as we discussed earlier, like the goat.

I'm waiting to hear from you fightin' Billies such as John, Brian, or Robert. Oh yeah, my nickname was Heavy D. There was a rapper named "Heavy D" at that time, but I'm not sure why it caught on as my nickname. The "D" was because they called me "Jon D." I think the "Heavy" was because of my deep philosophical thought.

My trophy collection is less than vast. Of the two I have, I'd say my "Offensive Player of the Week" trophy from 1991 is my most prized. I was (and am) short and chubby and played offensive guard for the Monticello Billies. We were playing the McGehee Owls. They had a highly recruited defensive lineman who played across from me and on the week in question, he didn't make a single tackle. I'm pretty sure he had mono or something, but at any rate it looked like I got the best of him that night and I was awarded Player of the Week. It's been almost three decades since then, yet as I write this I'm wondering, "Will any of my old teammates read this and send me a message like, 'Heavy D, I totally remember that game. You were awesome!'"

Our motivation for winning fights should never be for our own glory. Edward Perronet knew what to do with trophies. In 1779, he wrote "All Hail the Power of Jesus' Name."

I remember seeing one of the verses of that song in a hymn book when I was young and the image it conjured stuck with me.

Verse three says:

> Sinners, whose love can ne'er forget
> the wormwood and the gall,
> go spread your trophies at His feet,
> and crown Him Lord of all.
> Go spread your trophies at His feet,
> and crown Him Lord of all.

Like I said, Mr. Perronet knew what to do with our trophies.

What are you recognized for? Is it your slingshot prowess? Maybe it's your athletic ability. Do you have a great mind? Are you the next American Idol? Write down a couple of things people might praise you for.

Find a way to deflect that praise to the feet of Christ. You will be amazed how much better your trophies look at Jesus' feet than on your mantle.

"All Hail the Power of Jesus' Name" was written in 1779! That is staying power. Do you think they will still be singing any of Kanye's songs in the year 2258?

WEEK SIX

DAVID THE KING

We have spent our whole time looking at what happens when fighters fight. But as I am sure you are painfully aware, sometimes fighters hang up their gloves, kick back, and relax. As painful as this is going to be, I think we can learn a lot by taking a deeper look at the bitter defeat of the man we just saw lopping off the giant head of one of the world's most fearsome warriors.

Move forward in time about 35 years from the victory over Goliath. David has been king for a while. He has fought a few battles since then. He's probably in his late 40's when 2 Samuel 11 begins.

Read 2 Samuel 11:1 slowly.

Some people say that verse one is not implying that David himself should have gone out to battle. They say it's simply talking about the fact that kings would send their warriors out around that time. I wholeheartedly disagree. If it weren't for that last statement in verse one, "But David remained at Jerusalem," I might not feel so strongly about it.

Literally David, the great fighter, didn't fight.

It's so amazing to think about what motivates actual fighters to fight. Some bare-knuckle fighters are motivated just by the excitement of fighting. Others like Floyd "Money" Mayweather fight for the purse they receive. Although he was guaranteed a paltry $100 million for his fight against Conner McGregor, Mayweather reportedly earned closer to $300 million if you count all his earnings surrounding the fight. Now that is pretty good incentive to fight.

This is such a "guy" question, but would you fight Conner McGregor for $100 million? I'm sure your grieving family would enjoy it.

Enough about reasons for fighting. Our question is, "What prevented David from fighting?" Think about it a minute and write

The gloves on the cover of this book are hanging up. That's probably indicative of the gloves in many Christian lives. When you picked up this book, your gloves may have been on a hook. I'm praying by this point you are in the process of lacing them up.

It's always amusing to me that these tough guys are fighting over a "purse."

down what you think might have urged him to remain at the palace while his men went and grunted it out on the battlefield. It might be helpful to think of the reasons you choose not to fight sometimes.

I think David was tired. We are going to look at verse 2 tomorrow, but give it a quick glance.

Read 2 Samuel 11:2 paying special attention to the first half of the verse.

He took time out of his busy "lounging on the couch" schedule to take a stroll on the roof. This sounds like a guy who is on a break.

How tired are you on a scale of "Ready to attack the day" to "Don't wake me for 6 months?"

Ready to attack   **Don't wake me for 6 months**

|———————————————————————————|

Rest is not evil. As a matter of fact, rest is a spiritual discipline. God's first example for us was work. He created for six days, but his second example is no less important. God rested, and He wasn't even tired. God knows us better than we know ourselves. He knows we need a Sabbath.

The word *sabbath* means "to stop or cease," as in the way God stopped working. It appears David stopped or ceased his commitment to doing good. The Sabbath is not a break *from* God. It's a break *for* God.

Look at what God says in Isaiah 58:13-14

If you turn back your foot from the Sabbath, from doing your pleasure on my holy day, and call the Sabbath a delight and the holy day of the Lord honorable; if you honor it, not going your own ways, or seeking your own pleasure, or talking idly; then you shall take delight in the Lord, and I will make you ride on the heights of the earth; I will feed you with the heritage of Jacob your father, for the mouth of the Lord has spoken.

Listen, sometimes fighting to do what is right feels like swimming upstream. And in our exhaustion there is a temptation to grab the nearest air mattress, take a break from our commitment to God, and lazily float downstream. DON'T STOP KICKING! These moments aren't the times we need a break *from* God. These are the life-giving moments we have to run *to* God.

True rest is only found in Jesus. Embrace His words in Matthew 11.

Come to me, all who labor and are heavy laden, and I will give you rest. Take my yoke upon you, and learn from me, for I am gentle and lowly in heart, and you will find rest for your souls. For my yoke is easy, and my burden is light.

MATTHEW 11:28-30

Notice Jesus is talking to people who are fighting here. ("All who labor and are heavy laden.")

Then He makes a beautiful statement. "You will find rest for your souls."

Take a quick inventory of your soul. Is it in turmoil? Is your soul weary and troubled? Jesus says come to Him for rest. Get rid of every thing that is coming between you and Him. Sheep are safest near the shepherd. Draw near to Him and find rest.

Read 2 Samuel 11:1-2.

Look at the way the English Standard Translation interprets the first two words of verse 2. "It happened…" In other words, to paraphrase the ESV, "As David took a little stroll on the roof, there just so happened to be a beautiful lady taking a bath next door."

I don't think we can blame Bathsheba for taking advantage of a warm day where she made use of one of those bath bombs her husband got her for her birthday. It doesn't seem like this was some master plan devised by satan to topple the kingdom of David. Based on what I see here, this was just David being in the wrong place at the wrong time.

At the end of verse 2, in your opinion, has any sin been committed? If so, by whom? Circle all you agree with.

> **David should be at war, so yes.**

> **It depends on how long David ogled.**

> **Bathsheba is guilty for not going to Bed, Bath, and Beyond for a shower curtain.**

> **No, at this point it's all very innocent.**

In our time, if you do not live in a remote cabin on Mars, you are going to run into the occasional "bathing neighbor." Opportunities for lust or any number of other sins "just so happen" to us all the time. There's no way to avoid them completely.

Only punks blame Bathsheba. This study is for both sexes, but men: man up. Lead for goodness' sake.

I remember, when I was around 13 years old, finally mustering up the courage to tell my dad I was struggling with temptation in this area. This was before cell phones, the internet, or even personal computers. Pornography wasn't available to me, but that didn't stop the war from waging in my mind. I don't remember exactly how I communicated it to my dad, but I remember thinking, "All these girls are not wearing clothes underneath all their clothes." I wanted to do right, but it was just so tough.

I'm not sure if this thought was original to my dad, but he told me you can't keep a bird from flying over your head, but you can keep it from building a nest in your hair. This means David might not be able to control catching a glimpse of his bathing neighbor, but he did have the power to head back inside and play some Atari or something to take his mind in a different direction. I may have merged 13-year-old Jon and King David's stories there.

How well are you keeping the birds out of your hair?

> **My hair is nest free.**
>
> **I have a few twigs up there.**
>
> **An eagle just opened an apartment complex up there!**

I know this can be a struggle, but fight for control of your mind. Do like Job 31:1.

> *I have made a covenant with my eyes; how then could I gaze at a virgin?*

Our "hero" David doesn't seem to have much of a struggle. He sends for Bathsheba even after he finds out she is married. He has an affair with her, and she becomes pregnant. Things only get worse from there.

It's tough to be a 13-year-old.

By the way, this is not an exclusively male struggle.

84

Before we wrap up for today, pretend with me for a moment. Pretend you are David's conscience. You are with him when he gets up off the couch and heads out for his afternoon stroll on the roof. It's the moment he sees his neighbor bathing.

As his conscience, what would you scream (or whisper) in his ear?

"DAVID! SHE'S MARRIED! Her husband is one of your greatest warriors. Seriously?"

Do you think you could've convinced him to go back inside?

The sad truth about sin is there is always collateral damage. Your sin is not in a vacuum. It can hurt your friends, your family, and more importantly, the cause of Christ. David's sin and the attempted cover-up has far reaching and devastating tentacles.

When Bathsheba becomes pregnant David kicks into cover-up mode.
Read 2 Samuel 11:6-14.

Uriah is a wonderful guy. Actually, it appears he is more that that. He is listed among David's Mighty Men. You remember them.

David's plan to hide his sin fails because Uriah is such a stand-up guy. He then moves into phase two of Operation Cover-Up.
Read 2 Samuel 11:15-25.

Illustrious King David writes a letter to Joab, saying "Have Uriah killed." He then places it in Uriah's hand for delivery knowing he is so faithful, it will be delivered quickly and carefully to Joab.

Using a line, graph respect for David throughout his life.

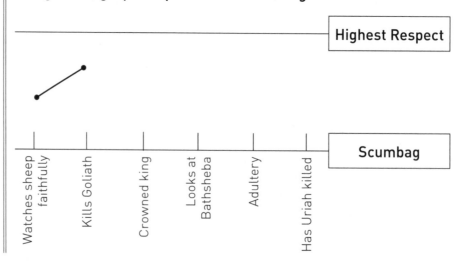

Who could forget Benaiah or Josh or Shammah?

Imagine Joab's face when Uriah hustles up to him with a salute and hands him the paper with the king's seal on it. Watch Joab unfold it and read those words, "Have Uriah killed. Sincerely, King David." David can never recover from a wound like that.

Bathsheba at least knew phase one of the cover-up plan. Even if she wasn't privy to David's murder plot, which she at least had to suspect, there's no way she could ever look at him the same way again.

Pick the most nagging sin in your life. Name three people your sin hurts.

1.

2.

3.

Don't feel bad if you don't name Jesus as one of your three people above, but our sin is most wounding to Him.

John 14:15 says, "If you love me, you will keep My commandments." Our disobedience sends Christ a message.

In the least crude way possible, write a cost/payoff analysis for David's sin. I'll help you with the "Things David Gained" side of the comparison.

<u>Things David Gained</u>   <u>What It Cost</u>

Brief sexual tryst

Is there anything worse than this?

Email me a few of the costs you came up with at jondforrest@gmail.com.

I'm so stinking curious to know what all you came up with in the costs column.

The costs go on forever, don't they? Sin does that. Actually, my columns were deceptive. David didn't gain a blooming thing. That's what makes sin, sin. God's commandments are for our good, always (Deuteronomy 6:24)! So sin, which is missing God's perfect mark, is itself a cost. Even the most seemingly enjoyable sinful things we do are done to our detriment.

Sin stinks. It promises so much and delivers only pain. Ask Eve. Ask David. Ask Judas. Ask Moses. Ask me! Ask yourself.

Sin is a terrible trade for what God has for you. What trades are you making?

avid must have thought his cover-up plan B worked. Sure it hurt, losing the respect of everyone close to him and killing one of his finest men and destroying his character and betraying the Lord of his life, but other than that it looked like he "got away with it."

He did not. Neither do we.

Read 2 Samuel 12:1-6.

Oh man, you see where Nathan is headed with this. Obviously there's no actual pet sheep situation going on. Nathan is setting David up and he falls head over heels right into the trap. David is steaming mad at the sheep thief. He's ready to kill the perpetrator for stealing the sheep and then make him pay back what he's stolen, times four, AFTER THE GUY IS DEAD.

Do you think you are like David when it comes to judging and condemning others more harshly than you condemn yourself?

_____ **No, no one is fairer than I (that sounds like Snow White more than a judge actually).**

_____ **Yes, I admit it. I'm all about justice when it comes to others and understanding when it comes to me.**

For example, you see a guy yell at his family hatefully and think, "That dude should be thrown in jail! What a jerk!" Sure, you yelled at your family the other day but that was different. You were stressed and nobody was listening and work was messed up and . . . you need a more grace-filled life.

Read 2 Samuel 12:7-13.

Can you imagine being Nathan's kid? He is a pro at this guilt thing. I guarantee you when he was done he said, "David, I'm not mad. I'm just... disappointed."

Write David's response to being busted.

What is your response to being busted? Is it more like Saul's response to Samuel when Samuel caught him in disobedience? Saul had been instructed to destroy his enemy, Amalek, completely. Saul spared the King and the best of the animals. When he met Samuel he kind of grinned and said "mission accomplished." When Samuel called him out on his sin, Saul had the opportunity to either confess or cover.

His response is 1 Samuel 15:15.

And Saul said, "They [the people, not me!] have brought them from the Amalekites; for the people spared the best of the sheep and the oxen, to sacrifice to the Lord your God; and the rest we have devoted to destruction." Then Samuel said to Saul, "Stop!" ESV

The phrase "the people, not me" was added for emphasis.

"They" did it! "The people" messed up. God knew better. God knows better. God is not impressed with our excuses. I'm sure the people did influence Saul's decision to disobey God. Even if our excuse has legitimacy, we are called to live above the excuses.

Write down an excuse or two David could've given to God instead of 'fessing up. I'll give you an example.

1. I just got caught up in the moment and felt a connection with Bathsheba.

2.

3.

Dear Saul, when you get busted in a deep, deep hole, stop digging.

David's response, "I have sinned," is the only path to forgiveness. Try it. Drop the excuses and bring your empty, dirty hands to Christ and let Him fill them with grace and mercy.

We have talked so much about fighting. Almost every day of this study has featured a person fighting to keep God first, but this is the page where we lay down our arms. You can't earn forgiveness by splintering shields. No number of defeated enemies placed on the opposite side of the scale of your sins could ever buy your pardon. The fight for your forgiveness was won at great cost. But man, what a victory!

Claim it today. If you are carrying a load of sin, say those three words to Jesus. "I have sinned."

Can I give you some good news? Not one single person who has humbly brought his sin to Jesus has been turned away. In John 6:37 Jesus says, "… whosoever comes to me I will never cast out."

There are no special words you have to say to find forgiveness. Simply, as specifically as you can, let God know you are sorry for sinning. Let Him know you are trying to turn away from those things and follow Him more faithfully. Contemplate His full and complete forgiveness. Once you grasp the amazing level of His grace and mercy, thank God for all He has done.

Use the space below to write out a prayer of forgiveness and thanksgiving.

This may be my favorite paragraph of this book about fighting, and it's the one place I tell you to surrender.

David has gone from "Fighter" to "Sinner" to "Redeemed." Redeemed. Say it out loud. My definition of it is to be deemed worthy again to enjoy the incredible Redeemer in an even fuller way than you did before you blew it. Sorry for all the fancy theological jargon there. You are redeemable.

If you've been carrying the guilt of unconfessed sin tell me "why" in the space below this.

I'm not leaving much space for your reply because there's really no reason to go another minute with distance between you and the Creator of the Universe who loves you enough to die for you. Pardon is free, full, and available. Follow David's lead with those three words, "I have sinned."

So now let's talk a little about undeserved guilt feelings. It can be tough to accept forgiveness. Even David had trouble with it. His lingering guilt is understandable. He did shirk his responsibilities, laze around, ogle a lady in her bathtub, call for her even after he knew she was married, commit adultery with her, attempt to cover the pregnancy, and kill the lady's husband. Guilt from that will stick with a guy.

Sometimes forgiveness seems too cheap. Monks used to wear hair shirts made of scratchy animal fur under their robes to make themselves miserable, or whip themselves for penance and to keep their bodies in submission. David beat himself up too.

Read Psalm 32. It's only 11 verses long.

When you read Psalm 32 it seems like David is overwhelmed with guilt and then confesses as if immediately freed from it. It wasn't quite that simple.

Thomas Becket was said to wear a hair shirt for years. As his body was prepared after he was martyred, the hair shirt was removed revealing swarms of insects.

Somewhere between verse 4 and 5 Psalm 51 takes place. Sin is a weighty thing. It makes sense that we shouldn't be flippant about it, but we also shouldn't wallow in the guilt of it.

This is how David described those guilty feelings in Psalm 32:3-4

For when I kept silent, my bones wasted away through my groaning all day long. For day and night your hand was heavy upon me; my strength was dried up as by the heat of summer.

Wake up your inner poet and describe how lingering guilt makes you feel, using some similes like David did.

Don't skip this. Give it a shot.

Put a check by any of the statements you can relate to.

❏ I really messed up, and I still feel the guilt of it.

❏ I keep carrying the same thing back to God for forgiveness. How could He keep forgiving me?

❏ Jon, you don't understand. I sinned BIG! I don't deserve forgiveness.

I know you've already flipped to a couple of places in your Bible, but just one more time turn to Isaiah 55 and read the first three verses. Think about what you're reading.

God says, "You thirsty? Hungry? Broke? Disgusted? Come to me and feast." Notice the last part of verse 3. "I will make with you an everlasting covenant, my steadfast, sure love for David."

God spoke these words through Isaiah 300 years after David ogled and killed and lusted. You are not more sinful than David, and God loved him so much He was still going on about his feelings for David 300 years later, not to mention giving them for us to read 2,700 years later.

The word God uses there to describe his feeling for David is "Chesed." It's translated "lovingkindness" or "steadfast love" in many places. We don't really have a word for it. It represents love that will not let go, even though it is undeserved and can never come close to being repaid. It's ridiculous love. God felt it for David, and He feels it for you. No, it's more than a feeling. He pours it on you. He embraces you with it. He's *The* Fighter. He fought to redeem you, and He won. Run to Him. Thank Him. Love Him. Live for Him like your life depends on it. Live to make Him known. Fight.

"Thirsty? Hungry? Broke? Disgusted?" That also pretty much describes the college experience.

NOTE TO LEADERS

Visit fightbyforrest.com for accompanying videos and a free Leader's Guide for facilitating group discussion for each week's lesson. Jon D. Forrest shares a great introduction for each week through video. The Leader's Guide provides practical insights for group discussions and suggested extras for each week.

To order additional copies of *FIGHT*
call 1-800-877-7030 or log onto www.randallhouse.com.
Call for quantity discounts.

NOTES

NOTES

NOTES

NOTES

NOTES

What is **D6**?

BASED ON DEUTERONOMY 6:4-7

A **conference** for your entire **team**

A **curriculum** for every age at **church**

An **experience** for every person in your **home**

Connecting
CHURCH & HOME
These must work together!

D6 CONFERENCE
ONCE A YEAR

DEFINE & REFINE Your Discipleship Plan

www.d6family.com

ONE HOUR
A WEEK

POWER OF
PARENTAL INFLUENCE